Ida B. Wells-Barnett

A Voice Against Violence

Patricia and Fredrick McKissack

Illustrated by Ned O.

❖ *Great African Americans Series* ❖

ENSLOW PUBLISHERS, INC.

Bloy St. & Ramsey Ave.
Box 777
Hillside, N.J. 07205
U.S.A.

Box 38
Aldershot
Hants GU12 6BP
U.K.

For Ann and Jerome Hamilton

Library of Congress Cataloging-in-Publication Data

McKissack, Pat, 1944-
 Ida B. Wells-Barnett: a voice against violence / Patricia and Fredrick McKissack.
  p. cm. — (Great African-Americans series)
 Includes index.
 Summary: A biography of the black woman journalist who campaigned for the civil rights of women and other minorities and was a founder of the National Association for the Advancement of Colored People in 1909.
 ISBN 0-89490-301-2
 1. Wells-Barnett, Ida B., 1862-1931— Juvenile literature. 2. Afro-Americans—Biography—Juvenile literature. 3. Afro-American women—Biography—Juvenile literature. [1. Wells-Barnett, Ida B., 1862-1931. 2. Journalists. 3. Afro-Americans—Biography.]
 I. McKissack, Fredrick. II. Title. III. Series.
 E185.97.W55M37 1991
 323'.092—dc20
 [B]   90-49848
 [92]   CIP
                                                       AC

Printed in the United States of America

10 9 8 7 6 5 4 3 2 1

Photo Credits: Schomburg Center for Research in Black Culture/The New York Public Library/Astor, Lenox and Tilden Foundations, pp. 4, 18; Department of Special Collections, University of Chicago Library, pp. 8, 15, 20, 21, 23, 27, 29.

Illustration Credits: Ned O., pp. 6, 10, 11, 14, 16, 22, 25, 26, 28.

Cover Illustration: Ned O.

Contents

Ida B. Wells-Barnett
Born: June 1862, Holly Springs, Mississippi.
Died: March 25, 1931, Chicago, Illinois.

1
Fever!

The **Civil War*** ended in 1865, and so did **slavery** in America. Jim and Lizzie Wells were freed. So was their three-year-old daughter, Ida. The family settled in Holly Springs, Mississippi. Seven more children were born.

Ida was sent to school. Learning was

---

* Words in **bold type** are explained in *Words to Know* on page 30.

easy for her. She liked to read, but writing was more fun. She made her parents proud. Besides being smart, Ida Wells grew into a pretty girl with honey-brown skin. She was also loving and kind.

Then came the fever! **Yellow fever** was a killer **disease**. There was no cure at that time. Many good people died in Holly

Springs. Jim and Lizzie were among them. So was their baby son.

Ida was just fourteen years old. Their Holly Springs neighbors wanted to take the children to live with them. But Ida kept her family together. They lived in the house her parents left for them. She got a job as a country school teacher to earn money.

The next year, Ida let other family members take the children. Ida moved to Memphis, Tennessee and got another job teaching there.

Ida B. Wells stood up for freedom when she was very young. In 1878–79 black men and women were leaving the South. They were losing their rights. Ida wanted to stay and fight.

2

First Fight for Freedom

After the Civil War, laws were passed that protected the rights of all Americans regardless of color. Blacks had the same rights as whites. They rode in train cars together, sat together in public places, and shared the same public drinking fountains. But by 1878 laws began to change.

Ida taught in a one-room, country school just outside of Memphis. She rode the train into town at the end of each week.

One day Ida bought a train ticket to

Memphis. She took a seat in the front car. The conductor said Ida had to move to the car where men who smoked rode. It was called a **smoker car**.

Why? She was black. But it was against the law to make people sit in separate cars because of their color. Ida would not move. The conductor took her arm. She bit him. He called for help. Another man

came. They picked Ida up and made her move. No one helped her.

Ida would not sit in the smoker car. So she was put off the train.

Ida was very angry. She was just sixteen years old, but she decided to fight for her rights another way. She would take the railroad company to court. She found a lawyer to take her case. Months passed.

Nothing happened. Ida learned that her lawyer had been paid off by the railroad company. She found another lawyer.

Finally, the case went to court. Ida won her case. The judge ordered the railroad company to pay Ida $500. It was her first fight for freedom!

The railroad took the case to another court, and this time, Ida lost.

From 1880 to 1900, states passed laws that took away black people's rights. Ida would always speak out against unfair laws.

3

Violence

Ida Wells went to Rust College in Holly Springs, and Fisk University in Nashville, Tennessee.

She still taught school in Memphis. Often Ida spoke out about how poor black schools were. She wrote for a newspaper, **The Living Word**. Ida lost her job because she spoke up about rights and fair laws.

Right away, Ida started her own newspaper, **The Memphis Free Speech**.

In many southern states, laws were

being passed that took away the rights of African Americans. Some laws made it very hard for blacks to vote. When blacks tried to vote they were beaten. Their houses and businesses were burned. Many times they were hanged. This kind of hanging was called **lynching**.

Ida wrote about these terrible beatings,

house burnings, and lynchings. She spoke out against the unfair laws that were being passed. Friends told her to be careful. Maybe she should stop. No! She would keep writing the stories.

Then in the spring of 1892, three young

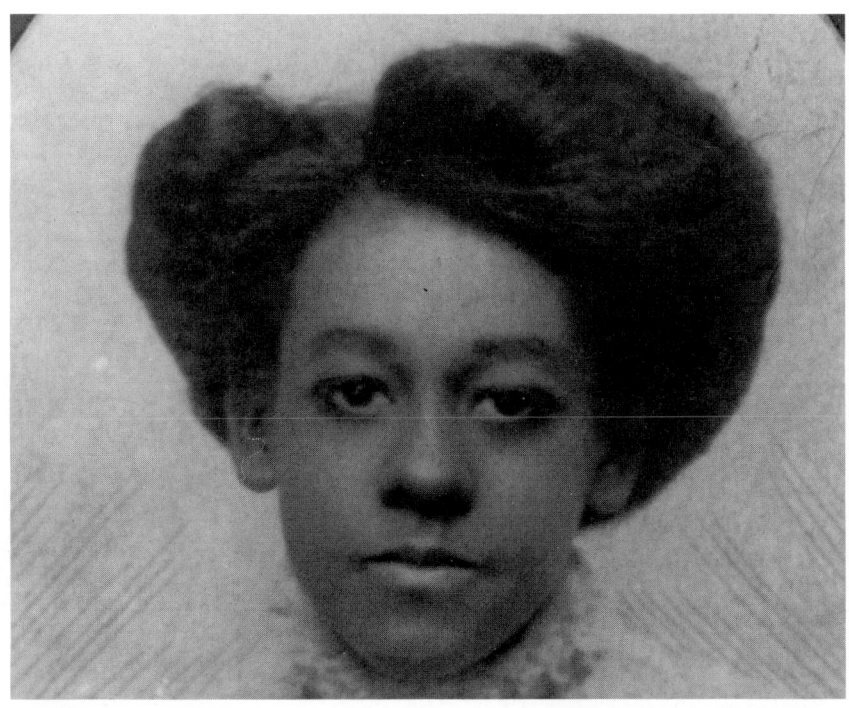

Ida had many friends and helpers. Maureen Moss Browning (above) was one of them. She helped Ida work for women's rights and against violence, too.

black men were shot to death. They had done nothing wrong. ". . . Say or do something," Ida wrote. Very few people said or did anything.

Finally, a group of angry men burned

the office of *The Memphis Free Speech*. Ida got away just in time.

Running wasn't easy for Ida. She wanted to stay in Memphis, and fight against **violence**. Her friends said, go North. Go where it will be safe to speak out!

And so she did. Ida B. Wells went to New York. Her work was not over. It was really just beginning.

SOUTHERN HORRORS.

LYNCH LAW

IN ALL

ITS PHASES

Miss IDA B. WELLS,

Price, · · · Fifteen Cents.

The year Ida wrote *Southern Horrors: Lynch Law in All Its Phases* (1892) 161 blacks were lynched in the United States. She would write many books.

4

The Struggle Against Violence

Ida worked for ***The New York Age*** newspaper in New York. T. Thomas Fortune was the owner. He said Ida "had plenty of nerve." Those who knew Ida agreed with Mr. Fortune's words.

In 1895, Ida wrote a small book named ***The Red Record***. It showed that thousands of black men, women, and children had been lynched. Something had to be done to stop the violence against black people.

Ida went all over the United States and Europe asking people to join her in her fight. Thousands and thousands of people joined her.

Ida met Ferdinand L. Barnett, a newspaper man from Chicago. They were married on June 27, 1895.

Ferdinand L. Barnett was a lawyer and a newspaper owner. After marrying Ida, Ferdinand helped with the anti-lynching work.

Many people wondered, would Ida give up her work? Not for long. When her oldest son, Charles, was six months old, Mrs. Ida Wells-Barnett went back to work. With baby Charles at her side, she spoke all over the country. She even spoke to the **president** of the United States.

Left: Ida with her oldest son, Charles, in 1896. Right: Ida with all four children in 1909, Charles, Herman, Ida, and Alfreda. Ida enjoyed her large family.

In 1898 Mrs. Wells-Barnett met with President William McKinley at the White House. She told him ten thousand black men, women, and children had been lynched since the Civil War.

The president was shocked. He made a speech against lynching. Still there was violence. The fight against it went on, too. Ida Wells-Barnett made sure of that.

Ida and Ferdinand with their children and grandchildren.

5

No More Lynching!

Ida was not the only person speaking out against lynching. Other women joined her. They formed clubs called the Ida B. Wells Clubs. *No more lynching!* was their cry.

Women could not vote. Ida worked for women's rights, too. But it wasn't until 1920 that American women were given the right to vote.

She was also interested in children's rights. Ida pushed for better laws that protected children from violence, too.

In 1909 there was a **race riot** in Springfield, Illinois. More killing . . . more burning. White and black Americans met in New York. Mrs. Ida Wells-Barnett attended. Something had to be done about the lynchings, beatings, and burnings. Out of that meeting came the **National Association for the Advancement of**

Colored People (NAACP). The NAACP was formed in 1909 to help work for rights through the courts. The NAACP also was against the **Ku Klux Klan, (KKK)** a hate group formed right after the Civil War.

For many years the KKK had not been very strong. But in 1915 the secret group started up again on Stone Mountain in Georgia. KKK members used violence

Some black soldiers were lynched after serving in World War I. Ida is shown wearing a button honoring "Negro soldiers."

and fear against people of color, Jews and Catholics.

Ida Wells-Barnett worked all her life to stop the KKK. *No more lynching!* was her battle cry.

When the spring flowers bloomed in 1931, Mrs. Wells-Barnett got sick. Two

days later, she died. Twenty years later, there was only one lynching reported in the United States. Ida's work had made a difference.

Ida B. Wells-Barnett is remembered as a woman who did much to stop violence in America. In 1990, a postage stamp was issued in her honor.

Words to Know

civil war (SIV-ill WAR)—A war fought within one country. In the United States, the Civil War was fought between Northern and Southern states.

disease—An illness or sickness.

Ku Klux Klan (KKK)—A race-hate group started after the Civil War.

The Living Word—A black-owned newspaper in Memphis, Tennessee in the 1800s.

lynching—An illegal hanging; a murder.

The Memphis Free Speech—The newspaper Ida B. Wells-Barnett began in Memphis, Tennessee.

National Association for the Advancement of Colored People (NAACP)—An organization started to help all Americans gain equal rights and protection under the law. The NAACP is one of the oldest civil rights organizations in the United States.

The New York Age—A New York newspaper owned by T. Thomas Fortune.

president (PREZ-i-dent)—The leader of a country or an organization.

race riot—Violence in the streets; violent acts against a race that has gotten out of control. ,

The Red Record—A book written by Ida B. Wells-Barnett in 1895.

slavery—The buying and selling of human beings.

smoker car—A train car where men who smoked had to sit. It was bad manners for men to smoke in front of women.

violence (VY-uh-lents)—Acts that hurt or destroy people, places, animals, and other things.

yellow fever—A disease that caused death at one time.

Index